THE BEST OF FRIENDS:

HOW TO LOVE YOUR SPOUSE EVEN WHEN YOU FEEL LIKE QUITTING

By

PROF. CHRISTINA DILL W.

copright@2022

<u>TABLE OF CONTENTS</u>

CHAPTER 6   54

INTRODUCTION

All heartfelt connections go through highs and lows and they all take work, responsibility, and a readiness to adjust and change with your mate.However, there are steps you can take to establish a healthy marriage or relationship, regardless of how long you have been together.You can find ways to stay connected, find fulfillment, and experience lasting happiness even if you have been in a lot of unsuccessful relationships in the past or have had trouble rekindling the flames of romance in your current relationship.

CHAPTER 1

LOVE, WHAT IS IT?

The kind of love that lasts a lifetime is true love, which is not a feeling but an attitude.It states, "I'm going to do everything I can to improve the life of my spouse with the help of God."

When you have this mindset, you speak and act in ways that are good for your partner and frequently elicit warm feelings from them.Warm feelings may also return to you if this person shows his or her love for you in kind and with words.

The fact that we have equated feelings with love is one of the great tragedies of Western culture.Love is more than just feelings.

Understanding what love truly is, is the first step toward becoming more loving.It's not only an inclination.It is a promise.It is a move.It's a choice.

"Falling in love" refers to those initial emotions like butterflies, heart flutter, and buckling knees.It's like reacting instinctively.It has no predetermined duration.If the relationship lasts for any amount of time, this brief honeymoon phase ends.

We can understand our confusion regarding love.We are enchanted by Hollywood.They want us to believe that two people can fall in love in a matter of hours (see "The Sun Is Also a Star" for proof);or days (see Titanic), emails (see You've Got Mail), and a plethora of other spellbinding methods.However, that is not real love!

After the spell is over, the honeymoon is over, and real life begins, true, genuine love begins.It's wonderful news!If we are aware that truly loving someone necessitates bending over backwards, we are prepared and do not give up.We never say, "Oh, no, it's over!"The butterflies? And my heart no longer flutters?How many butterflies?"

When you learn how to love, you become more loving, win your partner back, and have a happy relationship. This makes you a better spouse.It will be simple to implement genuine love in your relationship or marriage once you are aware of its characteristics.

LOVE AT FIRST SIGHT

A strong, intense "electricity type of feeling" that results from chemistry between two people is called love at first sight.It can be extremely thrilling and euphoric.It is similar to feeling "drunk;"The sensation completely consumes you.

Even if you only see them from across the room at a party, or get introduced when a new person joins the company you work for, or a friend brings someone new along for an evening out, others have described it as "an immediate sense of a person" and hoped it would last forever.It is an immediate reaction, usually based on a person's appearance, clothing, physical movements, voice, and how they look at you. One gets the gut feeling that there is something special about this person that makes them special, and you quickly get the feeling that they feel the same way.

CAN LOVE AT FIRST SIGHT LEADS TO A SUCCESSFUL MARRIAGE?

Sadly, the odds are not in one's favor that love at first sight will result in a lasting marriage.This is due to the fact that a long-term marriage will undergo numerous changes in its sexual and physical relationship.This is because of a lot of different things, like having kids, having health problems, having careers that have ups and downs, having periods of little or no sex, and times when partners just aren't on the same page.

"It is clear from the research that there is a general consensus that a couple cannot maintain their initial level of passion during a relationship."As a result, since love at first sight couples are brought together in a physical and sexual high so quickly, it is more likely to cause problems in the relationship to watch the natural sexual changes over time.

However, a spark can blossom into a lasting marriage if couples take the time to get to know each other before getting married.How this appears:It's like going on dates, either online or in person!that involve engaging in activities that complement each other's interests and individual preferences.Take the time to talk about your short- and long-term goals, fears, successes, and career and family plans for the next year and five years.

People really start to recognize each other's strengths, quirks, baggage, red flags, and everything in between during the honeymoon phase, which lasts about six months.

Therefore, you definitely have the potential to have a marriage that will last as long as you are able to work through that and maintain your composure.

However, don't underestimate the significance of that initial spark throughout all of this.When people come together under the'spell' of love at first sight, it becomes too easy to think that the rest of the marriage pieces will just fall into place. Despite the fact that a physical and sexual relationship is crucial to a marriage, it will never be solely about that aspect of the relationship.

Keep in mind that a long-lasting marriage is made up of many parts, not just love.

The difference can be made in healthy communication, intimacy, honesty, trust, and respect for your partner's life goals, dreams, and desires.That can't be sustained only by a strong spark; those take time, effort, and dedication.

CHAPTER 2

THE SPARK,WHAT HAPPENED TO IT?

You must be wondering about the spark's fate, right?

There comes a time in every relationship when you want to end it.

When you first met your partner, it might have seemed like you had all the answers to life.It might have occurred to you that you would never need any more relationships.However, you may now have the impression that you are clueless and are in desperate need of responses to the question of how your relationship has lost its spark.

Take some time to learn how to love someone when it seems like the spark has gone, though, before making hasty decisions.Although this is a difficult question, there is an answer—or answers.

Relationships can be difficult.

Relationships aren't always easy.

However, relationships can be fixed.
When it comes to relationships, you've probably heard the term "spark" a lot, but maybe you haven't thought about what it means.
Consider the literal meaning of the term "spark."A fire-starting bright flash of light and heat can come from this.Thus, the initial excitement of a relationship is referred to as a "spark," and it may even feel like your entire body is on fire and the future is filled with bright and exciting lights.
However, fire can overwhelm.It can quickly become out of hand.Additionally, it may burn out sooner than anticipated.It is normal for a relationship to lose its spark, but this does not have to be the end.It doesn't mean that you can't rekindle the spark in your relationship with your spouse with a little effort and time.

WHAT CAUSES THE SPARK TO VANISH?

However, despite those incredible feelings at the beginning of a relationship, you may one day wake up wondering where your passion for your partner went.As with a lot of other relationships, you might think that yours has lost its spark.If you've been married for a long time and find that you're telling yourself, "My wife doesn't love me anymore," there are a lot of different factors that could be at play.

The fact that it is perfectly normal for the way your relationship feels to change as it develops and matures is one reason why you don't feel it.You might start to feel less nervous as you get to know the other person better and feel more at ease around them.When they become a regular part of your life, you stop getting excited when they are mentioned.You accept them as normal.Even if they play a significant role in your life, your relationship is no longer novel or exciting.

It's also easy to get distracted by other things in life and forget what you liked about that other person when you first met them.There might be jobs, bills, children, chores, and a long list of other things that need your attention, depending on how long you've been together.Your emotions will begin to shift if you don't pay attention to your relationship with your significant other.

Additionally, you may end up focusing too much on the flaws that you had previously overlooked when those initial feelings wear off.When you do this, it's easy to forget everything that makes you fall in love with them in the first place, including all the good things they do.

WHY DO YOU LOVE ANOTHER PERSON?

It is essential to keep in mind why you love someone.When you rekindle the flame, you need to know what to build your relationship on if you want it to last after the initial stage of falling in love.

It won't work if you were in the relationship solely for the initial attraction and excitement it brings.For a relationship to endure past those beginning phases, you must have something greater to fabricate an establishment on.

TO LEARN HOW TO LOVE SOMEONE AFTER THE SPARK HAS GONE

This is the first step:

You need to reevaluate why you initially fell for them.

TIPS for LOVING SOMEONE WHEN THERE'S NO SPARK.

Get It Back

No, you won't be able to regain the same level of love you had when you first started dating.Notwithstanding, that doesn't imply that you can't keep up with any flash all through your relationship.

Even if they are brief or insignificant, focusing on the relationship in meaningful ways can sometimes be the key to maintaining or reclaiming the spark.For instance, you could leave a note for your significant other by their toothbrush in the morning, or you could bring a favorite snack with you to share for dessert or a late-night snack.Send them a song via text that makes you think of them, drop by their workplace for a midday pick-me-up, or arrange a traditional weekend date.You don't have to do everything at once;Make an effort to come up with a few small surprises that will brighten their day and demonstrate your love for seeing them happy.

Do your best to be thoughtful no matter what you do to surprise and treat your loved one.Planning a long date night might not be the pleasant surprise you expect if they are stressed out about work.An encouraging word and freshly brewed coffee in the morning might go a long way toward expressing your love.

If you take these small steps, your partner will hopefully follow suit and show you affection in return.It can be exciting and attractive to know that someone is thinking of you and trying to make you smile.It might even ignite its own fire.

Improve Your Ability to Forgive

Relationships Require a Great Deal of Work and People Are Imperfect.

It's normal to lose your enthusiasm.Additionally, partners are likely to say or do things that are inappropriate at some point.In any close relationship, mistakes and even intentional arguments are inevitable.You need to work on forgiving if you want your love to last beyond that initial spark.Holding feelings of spite will do nothing to help your relationship.

Also keep in mind that you may accidentally hurt or offend your partner at some point, and they must be allowed to forgive you.In addition to improving your ability to forgive your partner, you must be prepared to offer your own sincere "I'm sorry" when necessary.

Enjoy Your Time Together

Life is Busy, and It's Easy to Get Bored in Business.

At the point when this occurs, you begin doing the things that you "want to do" _necessarily offering your relationship the time and consideration that it additionally needs.

At first, you probably went out on dates and did things together that you both liked.However, it's easy to get bogged down in responsibilities and neglect your shared interests as a relationship progresses.

Make every effort to set aside time for you and your partner to spend doing things you both enjoy if you want your relationship to once again flourish.This will vary from couple to couple;Some individuals might like spending romantic evenings together at home, while others might like sports or activities outside.Volunteering for a cause you both care about can be especially satisfying.You might discover an entirely new area of interest to explore together.The thing that matters most is not what you do.What matters is the thoughtful quality time you spend together.

Learn To Communicat More Effectively In OrderTo Maintain a Relationship's Spark.

Indeed, improving one's communication skills can significantly contribute to a successful relationship.You might want to reevaluate how you communicate with your partner—or how you don't communicate with each other—when the spark goes out.At the moment, do you prefer face-to-face conversations or do they prefer time to reflect?Is every one of you portraying what you feel and changes you might want to make, rather than posting what the other individual fouled up and needs to change? Understanding requires communication, and especially in a romantic relationship that lasts a long time, feeling understood will enable you to care for one another more fully.Additionally, it will assist you in resolving disagreements without escalating into major conflicts.

You will be able to get the answers to the questions you are asking, like, "Has my spouse come to lose its spark in the relationship?" if you communicate with them.

Talk To A Therapist for assistance, which a therapist can provide.

There are those who mistakenly believe that going to therapy, whether on an individual or couples' level, means that a relationship is almost over.Therapy sessions that have assisted them in maintaining the health of their relationships have helped a lot of happy, long-term couples maintain their spark.You and your partner can learn important skills from a therapist that can improve your relationship.

Counselors and therapists frequently have the ability to provide responses to difficult inquiries like, "Why did my relationship lose its spark?"So assuming you're battling with cutting off a friendship since you feel like the flash is gone, converse with a specialist prior to racing into that choice.

A counselor or therapist might be able to help you see your relationship problems in a new light.They can assist you in sorting through your feelings and thoughts so that you can choose the best course of action.You shouldn't give up just because you think the spark has died out."Emotionally focused couples therapy resulted in sustained improvements in marital satisfaction," according to a recent meta-analysis of nine studies. This means that once the spark was rekindled, it remained strong.You can seek assistance from a mental health professional online if you believe that counseling with them could help you rediscover the spark in your relationship.

Because online therapy is adaptable, you can choose to pursue individual therapy on your own time or schedule couples sessions based on your and your partner's availability.Remember that relationship support is similarly basically as significant as the work you put into different fundamentals of your life, similar to home upkeep.If you would call a plumber to fix a leak, you should work with a knowledgeable and caring counselor to fix a relationship problem.

CHAPTER 3

ATTITUDE, WATCH OUT FOR IT.

ALCOHOLISM

Is there a way to stop being so dependent on alcohol?

You probably meet someone you know who is addicted to alcohol, and you may have the belief that as your love for one another deepens;Your spouse will undoubtedly improve.But what took place?
Isn't that why he can't get over it?
One of the most common addictions that people struggle with is alcohol dependence, also known as an alcohol use disorder.Alcoholism can have devastating effects not only on a person's personal life but also on every relationship they are a part of.Maybe, the most huge and most hindering effects come at the degree of closeness, organization, and marriage.Many romantic relationships are destroyed by alcohol, which also leads to divorces and a lot of family argument.From closeness issues, doubt, an absence of

correspondence to mishandle, absence of profound accessibility to monetary weight and the unfavorable consequences for small kids;

In a romantic relationship, alcohol abuse can have devastating effects on both partners, their children, and other members of the family.

RELATIONSHIPS AND INTIMACY AFFECTED BY ALCOHOLISM.

There are many different aspects of intimate relationships that are affected by alcoholism.Relationships can suffer greatly when people drink a lot.Intimacy is typically the first area that is typically affected.Alcoholism can have an impact on a number of intimate relationships, including:

Respect, trust, stability, affection, expectations, commitment, shared values, and codependency are all linked to alcoholism, as are verbal and physical abuse.Arguments, financial difficulties, acts of infidelity or, even worse, domestic violence are frequently the causes of deterioration in married or unmarried couples.Additionally, alcoholism reduces sex drive, which can exacerbate already-strained relationships and eventually result in divorce.

Prof. Christina Dill. W.

Mistrust and alcohol An individual's personality is significantly altered by alcohol abuse disorder, and as a result, they may not be recognizable as the person they were before they started drinking.Because of fear, shame, or guilt, people with alcohol use disorders tend to keep more and more of their personal information a secret.They begin to conceal information from their partner, such as where they are, who they are with, and what they did that day.Although concealing the truth to your significant other may initially appear to be an innocent defense mechanism, doing so will most likely eventually result in outright lies and mistrust.The lies a person tells to cover up their addiction become more elaborate over time as alcohol abuse progresses.It may appear to a loved one that all they are hearing is excuse after excuse for being late, disappearing, mood swings, the missing money, or the bottles in the bathroom that have been hidden.A relationship's ability to function normally depends on trust, which can be difficult to restore once it is lost.Fear and jealousy are two emotions that can frequently follow.Since honesty is required for effective communication, both parties may begin to experience feelings of loneliness and isolation, which may lead to an increase in feelings of sadness and resentment.

Getting help. The majority of alcoholism-related outcomes are negative, and broken relationships are frequently a byproduct.Professional assistance should be sought by anyone struggling with an alcohol abuse disorder in order to acquire the appropriate coping strategies and tools for overcoming this addiction.Since alcohol affects every aspect of the relationship, the majority of addiction therapists strongly recommend relationship counseling over support groups for their partner.Without trying to act as a therapist, it is essential for the partner to hold their loved one accountable and support them during their recovery.Accomplices and families are important for the excursion, whether they picked it, and merit help in returning to predictability.
The best course of action is, of course, abstinence from such a relationship.A nine saved by a stitch in time.Marriage is analogous to a padlock, whose key is thrown into the river once it is locked.Don't let love get you into a

situation or condition that will put your life in jeopardy.

IRRESPONSIBLE AND DISRESPECTFUL SPOUSE

When you say, "He's selfish, disrespectful, and irresponsible...I don't want to live like that but I don't want to end our marriage and our family if it can be saved," it's hard to get a better understanding of your problem.Therefore, congratulations on your clear understanding, which is actually a success.Before you know what's wrong, you can't figure out what to do.Whether the marriage or relationship can be saved will be the most important unanswered question in your description above.This will come down to how much self-centeredness, disrespect, and irresponsibility you can take from him while still feeling good about yourself and your circumstances.It is not a matter of whether the relationship or marriage can

last;The question is more about how much disrespect you are willing to put up with before it becomes preferable to leave than to stay.
It appears that you have repeatedly asked him to act in a better and more thoughtful manner in the past without much success;You will need to experiment with various methods of interaction with him if you want him to alter his relationship with you.It's possible that you'll need to learn how to be more assertive with him, not to back down, not to give in, and not to let him off the hook when he does something selfish (while doing your best to communicate in a rational way and not to complain or raise your voice).However, you will most likely encounter resistance whenever you attempt to assert your requirements.It would appear that whenever you push him for something, he escalates and threatens, knowing that doing so will shut you down.You can anticipate receiving more yelling and threats of divorce the more ardently you advocate for considerate, respectful treatment.You must be prepared for this.
This man knows your feelings of dread and uses them to hold you down.The challenge you face is to either stop being afraid or, at the very least,

to stop allowing your fears to paralyze you.He will lose influence over you when you stop allowing yourself to be paralyzed by fear, and the power balance in your relationship will unavoidably shift.He will either give in and behave better when you find your gentle but persistently firm voice and stop responding to his threats, or he will escalate to the point where it is truly dangerous to live with him.I trust that he is sufficiently shrewd to figure out how to think twice about, on the grounds that it is clear you would rather not leave this marriage.However, I hope you will have the courage to leave him if it becomes necessary to do so for your safety or respect.

   Divorce can be a sweet time in one's life.at least sweeter than what you seem to be experiencing right now.

Prof. Christina Dill. W.

CHAPTER 4

CAN DEPRESSION AFFECT RELATIONSHIP?

On the other hand, there is evidence to suggest that people who are in troubled relationships are three times more likely than those who are not to experience depression.Depression can be caused by relationships that are not supportive or happy.

Over 60% of people with depression, according to some studies, attribute their illness to difficulties in their relationships.Depending on the circumstances, depression may be caused by a relationship that feels punishing or dysfunctional, or it may be caused by the death of a loved one.Depression can result when a partner makes you feel like you're being blamed, ignored, or taken for granted, especially if this pattern persists for an extended period of time.Due to feelings of exhaustion, shame, and the sense that they are not worthy of anything positive, some people with depression have a propensity to withdraw from others.This can make you feel helpless and alone as the partner of a person who suffers from depression; however, this should not cause you to lose focus on your spouse.You need to push your partner to talk openly and honestly about how they're feeling with you.Discuss with them what you can do together to make them feel better and what they need from you to manage their symptoms.

However, it can be difficult to know what to do or who to talk to in order to feel better when you have depression.It can demonstrate that you are there for them and that they are not alone in this struggle by suggesting that you collaborate with one another.Instead, it's a problem that you and I can tackle together.

You might want to suggest making some changes to your lifestyle, like going for evening walks every day or starting a new hobby together.Learn everything you can about depression, including its causes, symptoms, and treatments, so you can help your loved one.You can conduct your own research or ask your partner's doctor for some sources that provide information about depression.Let them know that you still love them and are aware that depression is affecting their thoughts, feelings, and behavior.Reassure them that you will be there for them to help them get better.

WHY THE CHEATING?

What constitutes infidelity varies among couples and even among partners in a relationship. Infidelity is not a single, clearly defined situation.For instance, is infidelity regarded as an emotional connection without physical intimacy?What about relationships online?In the context of their marriage, each person and couple must define what constitutes infidelity.

REASONS FOR HAVING AN AFFAIR

Infidelity can occur in both happy and troubled relationships.Infidelity can be caused by a variety of things, including:
Unresolved marital issues, such as fear of intimacy or avoiding conflict Life cycle changes, such as the transition to parenthood or empty nesting Stressful periods, such as when partners are separated for long periods of time Personal dissatisfaction and low self-esteem also can play a role in causing infidelity.

Physical health issues, such as chronic pain or disability Mental health issues, such as depression, anxiety, or bipolar disorder Addiction, including addiction to sex, love, romance, gambling, drugs,
When an affair is first discovered, it typically elicits strong feelings and a sense of loss from both partners.The partner who was cheated on may experience trauma as a result of the breach of trust and obsess over the specifics of the affair.The infidel partner might be afraid of being punished forever.At this point, it's usually hard to think clearly enough to make decisions about the long term.

THINK ABOUT THE FOLLOWING:

Avoid making hasty choices.Seek professional assistance right away if you think you might physically hurt yourself or someone else.
Give one another room.An affair's discovery is always traumatic.As you try to understand what has occurred, you might notice that you are acting out of character or erratically.As you begin the healing process, try to avoid discussions that are emotionally charged.

*Seek support.*It can be helpful to talk about your experience and feelings with trusted friends or family members who can help, encourage, and walk with you on your journey toward healing.People who tend to be critical, judgmental, or biased should be avoided. Some spiritual leaders have received training and may be of assistance.You might want to think about going to a marriage and family therapist on your own or with a friend.

*Give it some time.*Avoid delving into the intimate details of the affair at first, despite your deep desire to comprehend what transpired.It could be harmful to do so without professional guidance.
Rebuilding a marriage that has been torn apart Coming to terms with having an affair will be one of the most difficult parts of your life.This challenge might accompany inner conflict and vulnerability.However, it can deepen and strengthen the love and affection we all desire as you rebuild trust, admit guilt, learn to forgive, and reconcile conflicts.
Consider these moves toward advance recuperating:

Still undecided.Take some time to heal and learn about the circumstances surrounding the affair before making a decision about whether to remain married or dissolve it.
Keep your word.Accept full responsibility for your actions if you were unfaithful.Stop the relationship and all contact with the other person.If the affair involved a coworker, you should only talk about business or look for a new job.

*Get assistance from multiple sources.*Seek the assistance of friends who are understanding and without judgment, seasoned spiritual leaders, or a trained counselor.Not all self-help books are created equal.Consult a professional for guidance regarding additional reading.

*Talk to a marriage coach.*Seek the assistance of a licensed therapist who specializes in marital therapy and has dealt with infidelity before.If you and your partner want to avoid divorce, marriage counseling can help you put the affair in perspective, identify issues that may have contributed to it, learn how to rebuild and strengthen your relationship, and avoid it altogether.

*Regain faith.*Create a strategy to rekindle trust and bring about reconciliation.Set a schedule and a procedure.Admit you were unfaithful and work toward genuine forgiveness.If your partner was unfaithful, apologize as soon as you can.Together, try to figure things out.
Moving forward: The reward may be a new kind of marriage that will continue to grow and probably surpass your previous expectations if you are both committed to healing your relationship despite the pain.

VERBAL ABUSE COMMON WARNING SIGNS

They Call You Names Negative

Name-calling is a sign of verbal abuse.If the name offends you, it probably came about that way.While some names are unquestionably mean, others more closely resemble sarcastic compliments.These might be harder to tell apart, but go with your gut.Verbal abusers frequently target their partner's self-esteem with "constructive" criticism.According to Peck, verbal abusers typically target their partners' insecurities and feelings of shame with their words.

Consider it a red flag if your spouse constantly criticizes you "for your own good."The most subtle form of verbal abuse is this one.

A form of abuse is using critical, sarcastic, or mocking words to make you feel bad about yourself—either privately or in public.These could be remarks about your intelligence, how you talk, or how you dress.The abuser often intends to make comments that make you feel inferior or ashamed.Equality in the relationship is not at the center of a partner's values when they use verbal abuse.In order to assert control over the relationship, they attempt to make their partner feel "less-than."

They Raise Their Voice When your spouse starts yelling without much of a reason, you might be worried that anything you say will make them angry.It is not a good sign if you feel like you are walking on eggshells and have to censor what you say in front of them.You won't feel safe in the relationship if your partner is emotionally volatile and shouts to intimidate you.

They Use Threats to Scare You

Threats to your life or body can make you afraid, even if they're empty.Never take a threat lightly.In a healthy relationship, you shouldn't have to worry about your safety even if your spouse claims they are only joking.If a threat prompts you to alter your behavior or makes you feel apprehensive, it's especially important to take it seriously.

If your spouse loses their temper, do they blame you for the actions they took or their subsequent behavior?Victim-blaming is a sign of verbal abuse that is frequently linked to narcissistic personalities.Your apologies for their actions may be the result of their deliberately convoluted explanations or reasons.In order to make you believe they never really hurt you, they might then be overly affectionate.

It is essential to keep in mind that people in abusive relationships do not always experience volatile abuse on a consistent basis.After an abusive episode, couples frequently reconcile and experience a brief "honeymoon phase."This piece creates emotional complexity and encourages victims to justify or accept responsibility for their partner's abuse.

They Dismiss Your Feelings

If your partner won't talk about things that make you angry, it could be because they want to avoid taking responsibility.Questions that are negative reflections on their behavior are brushed aside, and conversations about hurtful words and actions are terminated.Another form of gaslighting is this:Your partner insists that certain events "didn't happen" or that you are misremembering things, and your concerns are ignored.Gaslighting can make you question your own reality, which can lead to a cycle of blaming others for your problems.

They frequently report their accomplices letting them know they feel a specific way, which is going against what they truly feel (or think they truly feel;Some victims' emotional awareness is severely hampered by the abuse.

They Manipulate You

The persistent and ferocious use of threatening language may cause you to act or react in a way that makes you feel uneasy.At the end of a marriage, this kind of verbal abuse is common.They will say anything to play on your feelings and keep you in the marriage if they don't want a divorce.It's an effort to get you to follow their wishes, regardless of what's best for you personally.

You may find that you bury your feelings, try not to upset your partner, and work so hard to keep the peace that every day becomes an emotional chore. These are signs that you are a victim of verbal abuse. You may also have low self-esteem.You might feel down and wonder if you're crazy at times.You internalize your stress.You feel like everything is going on in your head as you punish yourself for your partner's actions.You might think that the verbal and emotional abuse you received was caused by you contributing to the relationship's problems, or that you didn't try hard enough to make the relationship happy or fulfilled.

You Feel Like a Different Person

When you are abused, it can affect your self-perception.You give up who you used to be because you get so caught up in the relationship and trying not to upset your partner.You let go of personal boundaries and lose your voice.It's probably time to get help if you find yourself using any reason to justify abuse in your relationship when you would never have expected to put up with it in the past.

It makes me realize how much they have had to repress their own feelings and emotions and have struggled to find their own voice in their life when I hear spouses say that 'at least' the abuse wasn't physical was a justification for staying in the relationship. Physical or not, the abuse is real.

You Feel As Though You're Walking on Eggshells

If you don't feel safe and secure around your partner, you might feel the need to keep your words private.There is never enough good in anything you say or do.It might be time to reevaluate your relationship and the role you want to play in it if you feel like you can't be yourself to the fullest.I start to look for indications of abuse or safety concerns when I hear people say that they are too afraid to say something because they are afraid of how their partner will react, in a way that seems to make them feel afraid.

HOW TO HANDLE VERBAL ABUSIVE BEHAVIOR IN A RELATIONSHIP

Abusive behavior is never justifiable.Advise yourself that it isn't your issue — and think about your choices for leaving when you experience it.You might not regard yourself— and your requirements—as being of any importance if the person you care about verbally abuses you and ignores your feelings.Are you?Pay attention to those emotions that are at odds with what you know is best for you.If you are being told in any way that your thoughts, feelings, and emotions aren't important, it's time to talk to someone for help getting into a healthier place.

Try to concentrate on getting help when you realize you are being abused.

If you are the target of verbal abuse, here are some things to keep in mind:

You can go to relationship therapy on your own or with a friend.

. Surround yourself with family and friends who can validate your experiences as a source of support.Talk to them about what's going on and how you're feeling.

Talk to your abuser about their hurtful words and explain why you find this behavior unacceptable.In a relationship, establish boundaries regarding what you will and will not accept.

When nothing else works, end the relationship or marriage.If you decide to do this, you should work with a lawyer who specializes in cases of domestic violence, keep in close contact with your support network, and concentrate on developing effective coping mechanisms.

After taking steps to leave the relationship, if you feel like you are in danger, go to a shelter.

CHAPTER 5

WORKAHOLIC NATURE

Couples are deprived of spending quality time together, truly engaged in each other's conversation, and sharing physical signs of affection as a result of work-related stress entering the home and being difficult to disconnect from.

Strong relationships can be hard to keep up at times, but when work takes precedence over building personal relationships, cracks can start to appear that may be hard to patch up later without conflict resolution strategies.Putting in a lot of effort is admirable and often necessary for success, but when life gets tough, it's essential to become a workaholic to get through it.

However, it is essential to reevaluate your priorities if you find that you work nonstop and never take a break.You must ensure that you are taking care of your mental and physical well-being.

If you don't, you might end up putting your job ahead of your health and happiness.

Prof. Christina Dill. W.

Your relationship or health should always come first.Keep in mind that you can only live one life.Make sure you live it in a way that makes you happy and content.

10 WAYS TO IMPROVE YOUR RELATIONSHIP WITH A WORKAHOLIC:

1.Don't ignore the nature of his work. Be aware of the pressures it places on you and your partner.Accepting you knew somewhat early what's engaged with his work and you've consented to it, it's absurd to anticipate that he should chop down his responsibility.However, if the situation changes, it is acceptable to reconsider.Be honest with him about how hard it is for you to cope on your own.This ought to be important to your husband, and if it is brought up in a constructive manner, you might be surprised at the inventive solutions that couples can devise when they collaborate.

2.Reduce your nagging

This is never a good idea. If you are constantly irritated or nagging, your partner will be less likely to want to spend time with you.Being considerate of his work and respectfully asking him to take a break without feeling entitled is much better than being negative.

3.Don't compete with other married couples. Just because your girlfriend's husband watches Dexter with her every Sunday doesn't mean that your husband does either.Keep in mind that you chose someone whose work might take longer than others'.Work with your own circumstance since examinations are exasperating.Also consider how much time he actually spends with you.Appreciate the opportunities you have if you travel to the south together every year and manage to sneak away to the cottage a few times during the summer.

4.Utilize his calendar and assist him in making his packed schedule as efficient as possible.
Ask if he would be willing to let you add important events to his Daylist.However long it doesn't feel like an interruption to him, this guarantees you can keep away from a contention over missed supper with the parents

in law, and your man isn't worrying about making sure to add it to his schedule.However, keep in mind that something is only a good idea if both parties agree on it; therefore, if he objects, do not force this idea.

5.Establish a consistent routine If your husband clings to his desk every night, make sure family time is a must.Going for a walk or making a meal together can be as easy as this.In this instance, complete transparency is required.Don't be stingy when negotiating.Be sincere about the amount of time you really require from them.There will be no room for resentment once the agreement is fully implemented by both parties.

6.Bring him a cup of warm tea and offer to give him a massage to help relieve his stress if he stops working for an hour instead of berating him for it.You can train your man to look forward to taking breaks by giving him good reasons to stop working.You are demonstrating to him why he shouldn't, not guilting him for neglecting you.

7.If you believe your man is neglecting his responsibilities as a husband or, more specifically, as a father, don't demand anything. Instead, act quickly and tactfully.He may not even be aware that he is neglecting his responsibilities.Workaholics frequently operate in a trance similar to tunnel vision and are often unaware of their surroundings.By having a productive conversation early on, you can help him tune in.Resentment and entitlement will only result in a counterattack if these issues are blamed and discussed.Let him know in a nice way if you want him to listen and understand.I also recommend recognizing that he puts in a lot of effort and being specific about what you want from him.

8.Try to make the time you spend together count whenever life throws you a curve ball. Be loving and impossible to resist when you're together if your significant other frequently works weekends at the office.Do what you want when he's at work and have fun.It is essential to live your own life independently of your partner's.

9.Recognize the man behind the desk Some workaholics simply have higher energy thresholds and require activities other than work.If you have tried unsuccessfully to arrange a romantic evening at home with your partner, consider dining out instead.He might only need the additional stimulus to calm down.Reminding him that taking a break from work will keep him from burning out is another tactic.In order to cope when things aren't going well at work, self-worth needs to come from other sources as well.

10.Set up a lunch date for the two of you If you want to surprise your spouse by going to the office for lunch, you should discuss this with them first.Your intentions might be good, but he might want to keep his personal life and work separate.Unless both parties agree, no idea is good.

SPOUSE WHO IS UNCOMMUNICATIVE

It is essential to first identify the areas in which you need to work on improving your communication skills before you can begin the process of doing so.

Here are a few warning signs to look for. Using passive aggression instead of confronting conflict head-on is an example of passive aggression.

This could look like this: making jokes about your partner's inability to arrive on time, scolding them for being late, and making fun of their choices are all ways to vent your frustration without actually having to talk about it.Even though it might make you feel good right now, it won't help you in the long run.

Avoiding conflict by merely avoiding it will not help either.When problems are ignored, it only gives them time and space to grow into bigger problems in the future.

Adverse speech When you talk to your partner, you should stop being secretly defensive or hostile. This is a sign that you have entered a toxic communication pattern.

Speech that is violent can include: raising your voice, blaming or critiquing, controlling or dominating the conversation.

5 TIPS FOR EFFECTIVELY DEALING WITH AN UNCOMMUNICATIVE PARTNER

Dealing with a spouse who refuses to communicate can leave you feeling frustrated, irate, and helpless.There are ways to deal with a spouse who doesn't talk to you.

Although these strategies may not immediately resolve your issue, they will put you on the path to establishing a more stable emotional foundation with your partner.

1.Don't spend too much time analyzing your partner's words or actions.When one person doesn't want to talk to the other, the one who wants to talk often starts obsessing over what's wrong.

Although a serious problem may arise over an extended period of time if there is no communication, many people experience brief periods of silence.It might not be related to the relationship at all.Numerous spouses frequently remain silent due to stress and exhaustion.

2.Carefully discuss it and convey your desire for communication without being threatening.Use affirmative phrases like "I love you and want the strongest marriage possible" as examples.I believe that communication is necessary for that to occur.If you attack and place blame on him by saying things like,what's the matter with you?It is likely that you will exacerbate the issue.

3.Demand for times of correspondence
   Demand brief, determinable times of correspondence.Some spouses are afraid that starting a conversation will result in a seemingly endless argument.Your spouse may be more receptive if you respectfully request a brief amount of time to communicate (ask them to set the limit).

4.Take stock of your own communication abilities.
She might not want to talk to you if you interrupt, are sarcastic or insulting, or don't really listen to your spouse.You might need to ask your mate how you might be a superior communicator.

5.Maintain healthy friendships and family ties.
It's bound to be depressing to look to a spouse who doesn't talk to you for emotional support.Having other positive connections will

assist you with being a better individual
inwardly.

CHAPTER 6

WHY DOES MY SPOUSE HAVE TOO MUCH CONTROL?

It's not always easy to tell when a partner is in charge.In an effort to "keep you in check," some individuals may display overt menacing behavior while others may resort to subtle manipulation.

Why some spouses become controlling Some people's controlling behavior may actually be a way to protect themselves from a difficult inner world.

When they're scared of what's going on inside, people sometimes focus on trying to control things outside.They might be afraid of being abandoned, worried about losing control, afraid of getting too close, having OCD in relationships, or not knowing what will happen next.

A person isn't always a "bad" person if they act in a controlling way.This may be a mental health condition's clinical symptom.It could indicate a personality disorder, unresolved trauma or abuse, or depression, for instanceHowever, this does not obligate you to accept actions that harm you or restrict your freedom of choice.There's help accessible for somebody who acts in controlling ways.However, you may not be responsible for providing that support.

You can keep things in perspective and see what really is going on by being more aware of the underlying reasons for their behavior:They

might be hurting.Furthermore, it is not about you.There's nothing "wrong" with you.
It is your right to be happy and free in all of your relationships.
Now consider these:It's possible that you'll rush out of hot water if you jump in.But what happens when you slowly heat up lukewarm water and step into it?
It may be difficult to initially recognize some of your partner's controlling behaviors because they are so subtle or appear so gradually.Some of them might become second nature to you.Then, you might realize that the water is too hot and hurting one day.
However, not all controlling partners act in the same way.Control can be subtly incorporated into your relationship to a variety of degrees.

The way you feel about these actions is the only thing that matters.
Do they make you feel uneasy, insecure, or tied down in some way about yourself or your life?This alone may be cause for concern.

THE MOST TYPICAL SYMPTOMS OF A CONTROLLING SPOUSE ARE as FOLLOWS:

1.The line between being attentive and feeling pressured blurs when they make decisions for you.

However, if your partner consistently makes decisions for you, it could be the latter.Controlling behavior is this.
It's possible that they take up too much time on your schedule or always insist on driving you everywhere.
They might also arrange things with your friends without first asking you, or they might paint or redecorate only to suit their preferences.
They might tell you that they don't like the way you dress, or they might start slowly "changing your wardrobe" by buying you specific outfits as gifts.

2.They are overprotective.

Caring for you does not mean controlling you; however, it may be difficult for you to distinguish the two at times.

If a partner questions who you've been with, gets upset when you don't answer the phone right away, or acts jealous of your friends and family, they may be overprotective.

They might also make the assumption that you are only at risk when you are with them, or they might demand that you consult with them each time you make a decision about your life.

A controlling partner might make sure you go to your doctor's appointments, make you a special diet, or tell you not to work with that coworker they don't like.

Any of these ways of behaving all alone probably won't make a difference specifically.But if your partner or spouse behaves this way on a regular basis and doesn't take into account your needs, wants, and opinions, they might be trying to control you.

3.They play the blame game

A controlling individual may have difficulty accepting responsibility for their actions.

When you confront a controlling boyfriend, you might find that they have turned on you in some way.Even if you don't intend to, you might find yourself apologizing for something.

Let's say, for instance, that you have been texting a close friend about the difficulties you are having in your relationship.Your girlfriend reads the private messages on your phone while you're in the shower, then gets mad at you for what they saw.

In order to avoid taking responsibility for their actions, they may shift the blame to you rather than admitting that they invaded your privacy in the first place.In a relationship, controlling behavior is evidenced by this.

4.They give you a bad review

This is more than just a careless comment here or there; after all, everyone has bad days. Criticism can take the form of making jokes about you in front of other people, making fun of your clothes, or always pointing out mistakes, like the one place you forgot to shave your legs or a little dust on the floor you forgot to clean.

Constant criticism has the potential to wear you down over time and cause you to act in certain ways to avoid criticism.

5.They micromanage you

A controlling romantic partner might try to stop you from doing things the way you normally would.They may:

tell you what to wear or how to wear your hair, pressure you to stay a certain weight, and try to control your finances. They might also tell you when you can go to work or school and hide your school or work materials from you. A controlling spouse might also exhibit this tendency in everyday situations.For instance, they might:

always inquire about your conversations after you hang up the phone; check what you just pulled from the refrigerator; supervise what you buy at the grocery store.

6.*They keep you apart from other people.*

Isolating behavior can be subtle, like not talking to you when you tell stories about other people or rolling their eyes when you answer the phone.

It might also be more obvious.

The amount of time you spend with other people, like friends or family, may be criticized by a controlling spouse.They might disparage your loved ones or claim that they have a negative effect on you.They might try and act in some ways that make rubbing when your companions or family are near.

In order to prevent you from carrying out plans with other people, they can also isolate you by requiring your attention during a crisis.When you choose to spend time with another person, they might treat you silently.

7.They gaslight you

The 1944 film of the same name is the source of the expression "gaslight."In it, a spouse gradually persuades his significant other to think she's terrible her psyche by doing things like darkening the gaslights and afterward imagining that he didn't.

You might be accused of being overly sensitive after a controlling spouse minimizes an experience, such as an angry outburst.Additionally, they might say something hurtful and then reply, "It was just a joke."You're making things up."This is blasphemy.

They might even lie to you, deny what they said, or tell you that your gut feeling is wrong.Sometimes, they might even suggest that you get help because they think you're losing touch with reality.

8.They attack your security

A controlling life partner might interest to see your new visit history, or they might peruse your journal while you're working.They might also frequently inquire about your thoughts and emotions.

They might keep track of your activities, like following you around in their car, keeping track of how many steps you take with a Fitbit, or keeping track of what you do on social media or when you search Google.

Additionally, they may present their request for your passwords as, "If you have nothing to hide, why wouldn't I have those?"Demanding your privacy is a sign of a controlling spouse, and you have the right to it.

9.They violate your boundaries

If you say "no" to something, your controlling spouse might try to get you to agree to something else.Putting you under pressure to change your mind or arguing with you about why you're wrong are examples of this.

This also applies to physical boundaries.For instance, you make plans with a different person and tell your partner that you won't be there, but your partner shows up at your house without asking.

HOW TO BREAK THE HABIT OF CONTROL

Acknowledging the issue is the first step in making a positive change.

The first step is to identify the circumstances that compel you to exercise control.Is it when they go out with coworkers?when they wear particular outfits?When they don't like you? Identify the feelings that arise after you have identified the triggers.Do you feel dread? Anger?Sadness?You will be better able to alter the negative thought patterns that are driving your controlling behaviors the more information you have.

"Overseas action" is one strategy being tried.Ask yourself what the alternative course of action would be if you were to resist the urge to engage in controlling behavior the next time it arises.For instance, if your partner is out and you feel compelled to call them 20 times, try sending just one text expressing your love for them or doing something distracting like reading a journal or watching television.

Experts concur that it can be very difficult to overcome controlling behaviors on your own because they may be deeply ingrained coping mechanisms that you developed as a child.If you're having trouble with it, you might want to talk to a therapist who can help you figure out why you have these instincts, deal with your fears about them, and find a healthier way to deal with the emotions that make you feel bad.You might also get help from a therapist with self-esteem and boundary setting, two important aspects of getting rid of control issues.

Imagine that whenever your partner doesn't call you back, you always feel uncontrollably anxious, which causes you to engage in controlling behaviors. "A therapist can help you explore these unconscious reactions."

Above all else, try to explain to your spouse that your overly controlling behavior is a curse, and work together as a team to help you change your imperious attitude.

Experts agree that changing controlling behaviors is well worth the effort, even if they are deeply ingrained.In a way, overcoming these tendencies is a powerful way to regain control of your relationship and life as a whole.That sounds so poetic.

WHAT GAVE IN TO A SPOUSE WHO WAS SEXUALLY ABUSIVE

Sadly, when we examine marriages marked by sexual abuse, we find something entirely different.We witness those who lust to satisfy their own desires at any cost corrupting sex.Sex in too many marriages is marred by dominance and manipulation rather than loving mutuality and intimacy.Conjugal sexual maltreatment is an expansive term that can envelop numerous intolerable and exploitive demonstrations.When sex is demanded, required, or taken with force, as in rape or forced sex acts, the violations are at their worst.The unwanted introduction of pornography or sexual implements, unwanted sexual activities, and peeking or spying are additional forms of abuse.Sexual abuse in a marriage can be coercive and manipulative.Even when a victim expresses discomfort or refuses, an oppressor uses unrelenting pressure or threats to force a sexual encounter.We must also make it clear what is and is not marital sexual abuse.The differences in their sexual appetites and levels of comfort are a problem for many couples.Couples who are in a good relationship are able to talk about and even debate their different physical desires without feeling threatened, rejected, or under pressure.Different preferences should be able to be expressed by spouses without either of them putting a demand on the other.Additionally, not all pornographic content is abusive.Both the utilization and the production of sexual entertainment is dependably evil, yet all the same it's not oppressive except if it's undesired.Evil behaviors that everyone agrees on are wrong, not abusive.Coercion is necessary for abuse.

Unrelenting pressure, callous disregard, unwanted acts, coercion, degradation, accusations of adultery, using sex as a bargaining chip, and technological abuses, among other things, are typical characteristics of sexual abuse.

<u>HERE ARE SOME SAFETY TIPS IF YOU OR SOMEONE YOU KNOW HAS BEEN THE VICTIM OF SEXUAL ABUSE IN A TEEN RELATIONSHIP:</u>

*Believe in yourself.*It is not, even if you are unsure or it does not feel right.

Avoid time alone and have a friend drive you home from events if you decide to stay together. Write down every reason for your own reference if you want to end the relationship. Break up by phone, email, or in a public place with witnesses nearby if you feel unsafe. Make your social media profile private and prevent the abuser from contacting you online. If you think you might be in immediate danger, call the police.

<u>HOW TO FIX SEXUAL ABUSIVE RELATIONSHIP</u>

A study that tried to understand domestic sexual violence and abuse in intimate relationships from a public health perspective came to the conclusion that the occurrence of sexual abuse in relationship has multiple consequences and that as long as violent behavior patterns may be accepted as a private matter, its causes and effects will be overlooked. It is necessary to involve efforts that reduce aggressive incidents in intimate relationships. Keep a detailed record of any threatening, menacing, violent, or abusive behavior.

It is not easy to end a sexually abusive relationship, but it is doable.Have a conversation in which you explain why you are hurting and what you need from your partner if you are willing to forgive your partner and heal from the cycle of abuse.

You can begin the process of going to individual therapy while your partner does individual work to learn how to overcome sexually abusive behaviors if the conversation goes well.Finally, you and I can start relationship counseling together.

It is possible to fix the relationship if your partner is truly committed to change and accepts responsibility for the harm they have done.

On the other hand, it may not be possible to fix the relationship if your partner promises to change but keeps doing the same things. In this case, you can continue individual therapy to help you heal from emotional abuse.

PHYSICAL ABUSE IN A RELATIONSHIP

It is real and occurs far more frequently than many people think.Additionally, it is life-altering and devastating.Most importantly, it takes place in complete silence.It frequently goes unnoticed by the outside world, sometimes waiting until it is too late to fix.

TIPS ON HOW TO RECOGNIZE PHYSICAL ABUSE

Here are some interesting facts about physical abuse in relationships and some facts about physical abuse that may help victims get the right perspective and help.

1. Physical abuse in a relationship is more than just beatings. Many people who are physically abused don't know they're in an abusive relationship.

This is because we are taught to look at physical abuse in a relationship in a certain way. If we don't see that, we start to wonder if the abuser's actions are really violence.
However, physical abuse includes being pushed aside, restrained against a bed or wall, "lightly" smacked on the head, dragged along, rough-tied, or driven recklessly.

2.Physical violence is the most obvious form of abuse in a relationship, but emotional or verbal abuse is often present as well. Physical violence is rarely the only form of abuse.
And it's a terrible experience to be abused by someone we thought would be kind to us and protect us from harm.However, a relationship becomes a living hell when we combine verbal and physical abuse with emotional abuse.

3.What counts as physical abuse in a relationship does not necessarily involve being harmed physically; however, many forms of verbal abuse can also be constituted in an abusive relationship. Physical abuse in a relationship typically develops gradually.

Additionally, emotional and verbal abuse can frequently serve as a startling glimpse into a highly toxic and even dangerous relationship. While a victim of psychological abuse can engage in a variety of self-harming beliefs and practices, physical abuse in a relationship typically serves as the gloomy culmination of a pathological relationship.

While most physically abusive relationships begin with demeaning and controlling behavior, not all emotionally abusive relationships reach that point.

Be on the lookout for the warning signs if your partner continually mocks you, makes you feel bad for their aggression, and tells you that you don't deserve better. They might be on their way towards turning out to be actually fierce also.

4. Long-term consequences can result from physical abuse in a relationship. A lot of research has been done to figure out what causes physical abuse in a marriage. Obviously, being thrown around or beaten has an immediate effect on one's physical health. However, despite the fact that they can also have severe and long-lasting effects, these recover. Physical abuse in a relationship can be

life-threatening for the victims in its extreme form, which is not uncommon.
Those who do survive experience a variety of psychological and physiological changes as a result of being exposed to ongoing violence in an environment that ought to be loving and safe.
Among the most common side effects for people who have been physically abused in a relationship are chronic headaches, high blood pressure, gynecological conditions, and digestive issues.
The psychological harm that comes from being in an abusive relationship is comparable to the harm that war veterans suffer, in addition to these physical problems.
Some studies indicate that victims of physical violence in a relationship or marriage are also more likely to develop cancer and other chronic and frequently fatal diseases.
Regardless of its duration, frequency, or severity, physical abuse victims in a relationship are more likely to develop depression, anxiety, post-traumatic stress disorder, or addiction.
Additionally, the victim is left without the protective role that our friends and family play

Prof. Christina Dill. W.

in our lives because abuse rarely occurs without
the victim becoming socially isolated.
5.Victims of abuse are well aware of this: it
seems impossible to leave the abuser or a
partner who physically abuses them.They can
be quite seductive and charming at other times,
despite their violent tendencies at times.
Abuse can occur during prolonged periods of
seemingly peaceful and contented
days.Unfortunately, however, it is highly likely
that a partner will raise their hands to you again
once they have crossed the line.
Some people do it in a few years, while others
seem to never stop, but it's rare to see one-time
acts of physical violence that never happen
again, unless they don't get another chance.

SEVEN STEPS TO HELP YOU BREAK UP AN ABUSIVE RELATIONSHIP WITH YOUR SPOUSE

1.Identify the Abuse

This is more difficult than you might think.
The victim may sometimes believe that the
abusive behavior is typical of a romantic

relationship.This is normal on the off chance that you were raised by oppressive guardians.You could also be being gaslighted into accepting their bad behavior by this individual.

Keep in mind that abuse can take many forms.Emotional abuse can be just as harmful, whether it comes from harsh words or a lack of attention.

Change is required if your partner's behavior is making you feel bad.Listen to what your loved ones, friends, or therapist have to say about the situation.They will try to give you a better understanding of what's going on.

However, in the end, you must determine what this individual is doing to your mental health.

2.Stand Up to Your Partner: Tell your partner how you feel about their abusive behavior and that you won't tolerate it anymore. This conversation can be scary.You might be concerned that this conversation will bring an end to the relationship.Perhaps you are convinced that your partner will respond with additional physical or emotional abuse.As a result, it might appear as though this discussion will be fruitless.But not always is that the case.

Your partner may, from time to time, openly acknowledge their shortcomings and promise to make an effort to change.Sometimes, partners who are abusive don't realize how bad their behavior is.Again, this may be their "normal" if they were exposed to abuse as children.Whatever the case may be, confronting abusive behavior is a crucial first step in putting an end to it.Be firm when providing this feedback.They need to know that you mean it.You might have to give an ultimatum, despite how scary it may seem.because you don't deserve an abusive relationship; you deserve a healthy one.Either you leave or the abuse stops. However, you are not required to be aggressive when providing this feedback.Instead of focusing on the individual, focus on the behavior.Tell your partner that you love them but can't stand their behavior.When feedback is given in this manner, people are more likely to hear it and accept it.

Abusers are more likely to become defensive, aggressive, or emotionally closed down when they receive feedback that is focused on them as individuals.

3.It is impossible to repair the relationship if the abuser refuses to acknowledge their shortcomings.
Yes, it is possible for your partner to say they will change and then do so.
However, it's also possible that they'll promise nothing in order to silence you.
You might observe a brief change in their behavior—perhaps long enough to prevent you from leaving immediately—only to see the pattern return shortly thereafter.
They will agree to see a therapist or another mental health professional if they are serious about getting better.
This should be recommended to them because it can be difficult to overcome the emotional barriers that lead to abusive behavior on one's own.

*4.Stop the cycle of emotional abuse in which the abuser causes harm to their partner.*The partner allows it to occur.The abuser goes on.That is the pattern of psychological mistreatment.
Be willing to let go of your part in this cycle in order to break it.

You will frequently feel as though it is simpler to continue the cycle.You might try to justify this by making excuses for them, attempting to give them endless last chances, and telling yourself that true love never came easy.
If you'd like, do that.Just be aware that the abuse cycle will almost certainly continue until you break it.Yes, if their behavior doesn't change, that means actually leaving them.

5.Know What Makes Someone Abusive
Before you can fix an abusive relationship
 Both parties need to know that an abusive person can change.
This unhealthy outlook on relationships was fostered.A healthier child can also be nurtured. When the abuser chooses to work with a therapist who is trained to comprehend and employ techniques to shift the abusive thoughts in their mind, this nurturing process is so much simpler.
The difficult part is:This process takes time to complete.To overcome this, patience and hard work are required.Even after the abusive partner has started therapy, there might be mistakes.

It is possible to end a toxic relationship if you are both determined enough to do so. However, there may be difficulties along the way.

6.Heal from your abuse

If you want to try to get out of an abusive relationship and into one that is healthy, you need to heal as well.

Investing in therapy as well is a smart move.A specialist will assist you with tending to your sentiments and let go of any enduring disdain held towards your accomplice.

They help you figure out why you were willing to let a toxic relationship grow in the first place, which may be even more important.Together, you can work on improving your self-esteem, learning how to build healthy relationships, and regaining trust.Anything you require.

This is an important step to take to help you avoid having the same issues with your current or future partners again.

7.Leave them if there is no progress

This may be the most difficult step.

You will want to stay if you love your partner.They will never let you down.You should give them credit for their excuses.You will persuade yourself that you still require one another.You won't accept the damage they are doing to you over the long term.

If the abusive partner is gaslighting you, this is especially true.Perhaps they are so manipulative that you believe you are the one in need of assistance.

However, the most typical circumstance is:Both partners must end their relationship in order to heal.

Yes, it is noble to remain and assist an abusive partner in overcoming their issues.However, the spouse must prioritize themselves at some point if the situation is not improving.

Abusers frequently wait until they lose their partner before changing.In such instances, it is in everyone's best interest to end the relationship.

When domestic violence is involved, this is especially true.If you don't break up with that person right away, you could end up in the hospital and they could end up in prison.At this point, it might seem impossible to end your relationship.But you can work through this and live a happier life with the help of your loved ones and/or a therapist.

<u>CONCLUSION</u>

What makes a relationship healthy?

You want a healthy and loving relationship, right? Then, *love yourself first!*

Every relationship is one of a kind, and people get together for a variety of reasons.Having a common objective for exactly what you want the relationship to be and where it should go is one of the characteristics of a healthy relationship.And you won't be able to find out that information unless you talk to your partner honestly and deeply. Notwithstanding, there are additionally a few qualities that most solid connections or Relationships share practically speaking.Regardless of the goals you're working toward or the challenges you're facing together, knowing these fundamental principles can help keep your marriage or relationship meaningful, exciting, and fulfilling.

You remain in close emotional contact with one another

You make the other person feel loved and happy.Being loved and feeling loved are two different things.When you feel loved, you feel accepted and appreciated by your partner, as if they truly understand you.Some marriages or relationships remain peacefully coexisting without the partners developing an authentic emotional connection.Despite the union's apparent stability, a lack of ongoing involvement and emotional connection only serves to deepen the gap between the two parties.

You don't shy away from disagreement(respectful)

Some couples discuss their disagreements quietly, while others may raise their voices and shout.However, the key to a healthy marriage or relationship is not to be afraid of conflict.You need to be able to resolve conflict without being humiliated, degraded, or insisting on being right, and you need to feel safe expressing things that bother you without fear of retaliation.

You maintain interests and relationships outside of work

There is no one person who can satisfy all of your requirements, despite what romantic movies and novels claim.In point of fact, placing an unhealthy amount of expectation on your partner can strain the relationship.It is essential to maintain your own identity outside of the relationship, maintain connections with family and friends, and maintain your hobbies and interests in order to stimulate and enrich your marriage or romantic relationship.

You speak honestly and openly
A key component of any relationship or marriage is effective communication.It can increase trust and strengthen the bond between you and your spouse when both parties are aware of what they want out of the relationship and feel at ease expressing their requirements, anxieties, and aspirations.
Beware that three stages of love comprises of *Lust, Attraction and Attachment.* When love leads to attachment,it is called compassionate love; A committed love that is characterized by feelings of calm, security, social comfort and

emotional union. A compassionate love will never fail. *Strive for it.*
 Go live a happy marriage with your spouse.

1